The First Siberians

by Howard Sochurek

Photography by
Howard Sochurek
and
John deVisser

EMC Corporation
St. Paul, Minnesota

Library of Congress Cataloging in Publication Data

Sochurek, Howard.
    The first Siberians.
    (His The new Siberia, book 4)
    SUMMARY: Describes the cultural heritage and daily lives of four tribal groups
inhabiting Siberia.
    1. Ethnology — Siberia — Juvenile literature. [1. Ethnology — Siberia. 2. Siberia
— Social life and customs] I. De Visser, John, illus. II. Title. III. Series.
HN530.S5S62 bk. 4 [DK758] 915.7s [915.7'03]
ISBN 0-88436-002-4   73-15629
ISBN 0-88436-003-2 (pbk.)

Published 1973
Published by EMC Corporation
180 East Sixth Street
St. Paul, Minnesota 55101
Printed in the United States of America
0 9 8 7 6 5 4 3 2 1

THE NEW SIBERIA

The New Russians
Siberia at Work
Lifelines for the New Frontier
The First Siberians

People From an Ancient Past

The Russian Cossacks first pushed into Siberia in the 16th century. They found many different native groups who already called the great land their home. The Cossack armies thought these peoples were primitive compared to the civilized society of Russia. But in fact, these tribal groups had a history that went back thousands of years.

There is still disagreement about the origins of these first Siberians. But most archaeologists believe the first Siberian settlers were physically like the first Europeans of the Second Stone Age.

Remains of early village life have been found fifty miles from Irkutsk on a branch of the Angara River. In 1928, while digging a cellar, a peasant in the village of Malta found a shelter built of animal bones. Mammoth tusks, skulls, and thighs had been used to support a roof made of reindeer antlers.

In the second century B.C. the Huns invaded Siberia and conquered the Siberian tribes in the Malta area. From the Huns the native hunting tribes learned cattle breeding skills.

The Huns in turn were conquered by the Turks. But later, the Turkish empire fell to the Chinese. In the early thirteenth century the armies of Genghis Khan swept over the Siberian land on horse, destroying and killing as they went. Some tribes fled the invaders and were

The building at the left was part of an early Cossack fortress. This wooden tower has been preserved on the grounds of the local Yakutsk museum. It was built in 1632 when the first Russian adventurers came to win Russian control over the Yakuts.

pushed to the Arctic Sea. Others were destroyed. And for three centuries the Mongols ruled Siberia.

The present-day area of Siberia is the home of over twenty tribal groups. Some of the earliest groups were the ancestors of the present-day Yakuts and Buryats. After the Iron Age they became linked with China, Mongolia, and Central Asia as they developed. Other groups, like the Yukagirs and Evenki, lived in the *tundra* and Arctic regions. They made little foreign contact and thus were slow to progress. Even today these groups remain somewhat more primitive.

The stream of Russians that started coming into Siberia in 1582 from west of the Urals has today become a flood. As a result of this immigration, there is now a fifty-fifty population balance between the "first Siberians" and the "New Siberians." Contact with the Russians has introduced the native peoples to an advanced culture and civilization.

But the minority groups of Siberia are making their own important contribution in a time of great change and development. Because of their remoteness from the bigger centers of population, some may still be described as primitive. But they know the ways of the land, and they have long known how to meet its challenging demands. Without them and their active help, the development of modern Siberia would be impossible.

A native Evenki herdsman harnesses a reindeer before hitching the animal to a sled. On the tundra, the reindeer is used much as a horse is for transportation.

This pretty girl in Magadan has a Russian mother and an Eskimo father. Though some mixed marriage exists in Siberia, it is not common. Many of the first Siberians are holding to their customs and traditions and they are slow to change.

The Buryats

With a population of nearly 800,000, the Buryats are one of the largest native groups in Siberia. The Buryat Republic is located in south central Siberia, on the border of Mongolia. The Buryat people are Buddhist in religion and Mongol in appearance. They have long had cultural ties with Mongolia and China.

Once the Buryats were a nomadic people, roaming the huge *steppe* with their herds of sheep and horses. Under Soviet rule they have become settled, while remaining separate. Driving through the countryside you will find first a Buryat village, then, a few miles down the road, a Russian village. The villages look almost the same with their one-room log houses and stone chimneys belching white smoke from wood fires.

But there is a difference. In the yard of a Buryat house sits a large, skin-covered tent called a *yurt.* Yurts are round with a domed top. They are formed by a framework of wood. They are left-over from the nomadic days, and are still used on the range as summer houses. The Buryats milk their horses and make wine from the milk of their cows. Their greatest food delicacies are fermented mare's milk and sheep's intestines stuffed with dried blood.

There are many pleasant things for the traveler in the Buryat Republic to enjoy. One is the charm, warmth, and hospitality of the Buryat people. They are friendly and helpful people. If your jeep gets stuck in midstream after going through the ice, the Buryats will willingly jump into the freezing water to get you going again. They love a joke and will keep you up half the night singing American songs they don't understand. They have wise proverbs like: "A camel does not notice its hump, nor a man his drawbacks;" or another: "A mountain wears down a horse and anger wears down a man."

The Buryats love to talk. And they are anxious to learn. One night I was huddled in a yurt sitting on the floor and sipping *kumiss,* which is fermented mare's milk. The conversation turned to America. My host asked, "How many camels do you have in America?" Other questions included, "Are there any taxicabs in New York City?" and, simply, "How did you get here?"

Today most Buryats live in industrialized cities like the capital at Ulan-Ude, where factories turn out locomotives, canned meats, and glass products. Other Buryats are members of State farms which raise sheep and cattle or grow wheat and hay.

Dressed in a huge *yak*-skin coat and a fur cap, a Buryat herdsman in the Selenga Valley, braves the fifty-below temperatures. He tends his herd on the Banner of Lenin collective farm. Buryats, once nomads, now live in log cabin villages.

11

In the two-room cabin of Chimit Gomboyev, foreign visitors are feasted with bread, meat, and berries. Chimit raises a herd of 600 sheep. This year he received a bonus of 2,800 rubles, about $3,500, for fulfilling the State plan. He raised just as many sheep as the government wanted him to. His cabin includes electricity, a television set, and a refrigerator. All were recently purchased.

Herdsmen follow their sheep on foot as well as on Siberian pony. This collective farm has 45,000 head of sheep scattered over the country in 50 different range camps.

The only State theater in eastern Siberia is in the Buryat capital city of Ulan-Ude. Here both native opera and ballet are performed.

In the theater's main hall Klara Mikhailovna, a Buryat opera singer, poses before an empty house. Many Buryats like Klara have adopted Russian names. As an opera singer, she has been given the highest honor of the Buryat theater: the title of People's Artist.

This is a performance by the Buryat National Ballet Company in the State Theater at Ulan-Ude. The ballet tells the story of a popular folk hero. Siberian folktales are the basis for stories, songs, ballets, and operas.

Dashinima Dugarov is the leading landscape artist in Ulan-Ude. He works on assignment from the State and sells his paintings to the State. There is no public market for art works in the USSR. Paintings are hung in museums and public buildings, but seldom in private homes.

Buryats are practicing Buddhists. Their religious leader is the Dalai Lama of Tibet. The chief lama of Buryatia is 77-year-old Gomboy Gomboyev. He was photographed at the Ivolginsky Monastery. There are over 400 lamas in the Buryat Republic.

A symbol of strength and power, a concrete tiger guards the entrance at Ivolginsky Monastery. Thirty of the 400 lamas in Buryatia live and worship here. Young Buddhists are sent to Outer Mongolia for training as monks. Ten are now studying there, and will keep the faith alive when they return home.

Three old visiting monks attend the "New Year" services at the monastery. The monks recite the scriptures for three hours, three times daily. Each monk, or lama, lives in a small wooden house inside the monastery. Support comes from the Buryat families who give an average of 80 rubles, $100, to the monastery each year.

The main entrance to the Buddhist Temple at Ivolginsky Monastery follows the architecture of ancient Buddhist buildings in Tibet and China. Inside are huge golden statues of the Buddha, the saintly founder of the Buddhist religion.

17

The Yakuts

"Yakutia," in the Yakut language, means "Land of Eternal Snow." Yakutia is larger than any of the other fifteen Union Republics in the Russian Federation. The Yakuti tribes make up the second largest native group in Siberia. They are an ancient people, and today they number over half a million.

Yakutia itself covers 1,210,000 square miles of land area and is located in central Siberia. The land contains large forests, but a large part of it is also treeless tundra.

Like the rest of Siberia, Yakutia today is becoming industrialized. Yakut mines near Aldan produce one-fourth of the Soviet nation's gold. Recently, huge new natural gas fields have been located at Vilyuysk. These too will soon be developed.

Before the Russians came to Siberia, the Yakuts were a hardy, self-contained people. They lived in cold isolation in small scattered villages. Many made their homes in round, skin-covered tents called yurts. They earned their living by hunting, fishing, trapping, and reindeer herding.

In the old days the Yakuts were entertained by wandering story tellers called *Olonkhosuts.* These men traveled about spinning fantastic tales in verse. Tribesmen would gather to listen in wonder to the adventures of Nurgun. Nurgun was the one-eyed, one-legged, one-armed giant who roamed the Arctic ice land. Other tales told of terrible battles with the primitive Gooturs, who could fell an elk with a blow of their fist or crush a rock in their grip.

The storytellers would sit around a wood fire talking all through the night. They would invent new and even more exciting stories as they talked. By changing the rhythm and tone of voice, heroes, old women, evil spirits, or even a young lover could be portrayed. All of the stories seemed quite real to the early Yakuts. The tales fed the hopes and dreams of the quiet, friendly tribesmen.

The temperatures in Yakutia are among the coldest in the world. An official low temperature of 97.8 degrees below zero has been recorded. During the long polar winters the sun does not rise above the horizon for eighty days, and people walk on a *permafrost* a mile deep.

In recent years many Yakuts have moved from the *taiga* to the town. A few work at digging mines, building power stations, and drilling for gas and oil. But most Yakuts still follow the jobs that use traditional skills: carving, leather crafts, carpentry, and woodworking. As one Yakut put it: "Our people are growing gently into the twentieth century."

Smiling Yakut school girls in the town of Pokrovsk near Yakutsk. Most Yakut children, unlike their parents, know and speak Russian. But their native language is spoken in the home.

The Yakuts are proud of their culture. They want to preserve their native heritage. They don't want to become cogs in the technical machine that Soviet society seems determined to create. The Yakuts are not being pushed or herded easily. But as a Yakut artist told me, "When the blizzard lashes the taiga only a fool tries to face it and struggle with its power."

The Soviet drive to industrialize Siberia is whirling through Yakutia today. And the Yakuti people may find its power too strong to resist.

Native students at the University of Yakutsk show great ability and intelligence. Some go on to important jobs in industry and science.

At the University of Yakutsk, young native draftsmen learn town planning and civil engineering. This is the northernmost university in the Soviet Union. It has nine schools, including a school of medicine.

The Yakuts love the far north country, and over many centuries they have adapted to the harsh surroundings. For this reason, they are the best fitted to help in developing this area of Siberia. But modern technology requires people who are educated in space-age skills. This university provides the training for qualified young Yakuts.

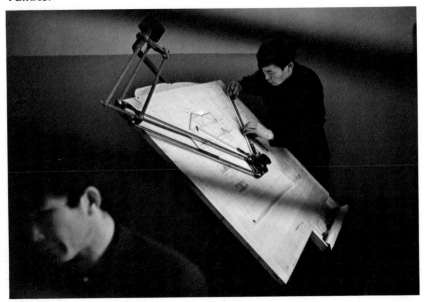

A pretty Yakut girl spends a Sunday afternoon walking along the Angara River in the town of Irkutsk. She attends medical college in Irkutsk and wants to serve her countrymen in the far north. After a six-year course she will return to Sangara as a doctor. There she hopes to work at a hospital on the Lena River.

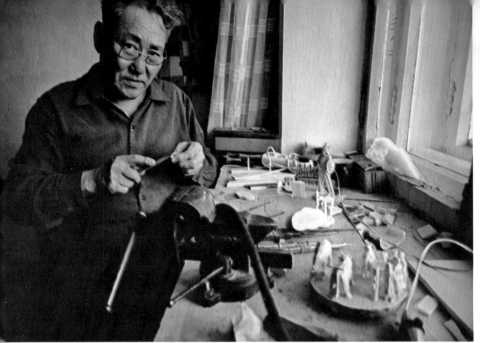

Many Yakuti people have a natural ability in art like this carver, Terenti Ammossov. He uses ivory from mammoth tusks that have been long buried in the permafrost of the area. Mammoths were huge prehistoric animals. Thousands of these two-tusked animals have been found in Siberia's frozen ground. Sometimes their meat, frozen deep in the earth for millions for years, can still be eaten.

One of the great weekend pleasures during the short fall in Yakutia is hunting in the taiga. The custom is to kill the game, skin it, roast it, and eat it immediately. This member of the Writer's Union in Yakutsk is enjoying some *shashlik*. Shashlik is a mixture of meat and vegetables roasted on an open fire. It is something like *shish kebab,* a Middle Eastern dish now popular in many countries.

A Russian harbor master and a Yakuti poet, close friends, pose for a portrait in Yakutsk.

The Soviet State is concerned about its minority groups. Many problems remain unsolved in providing equal opportunities for the native people.

Mrs. Aleksandra Ovchinnikova is President and Chief Executive of the Yakutsk Republic. She is also a member of the Presidium of the USSR. She is the daughter of poor, uneducated Yakut cattle breeders. She took her higher education by correspondence courses and now holds a degree in history.

She is trying to preserve the native culture of the Yakuts. But she also works hard for Siberian development plans. On her desk is a sign which reads, "A willing horse may lead a good life, but the driver leads a better one."

Yakut women hold other government jobs in the Republic. This lady is a research scientist at the Permafrost Institute in Yakutsk. The school is solving permafrost problems and obtaining information about the frozen earth. It has developed new road surfacing materials and new construction methods for high-rise buildings.

A recent problem arose in Yakutsk when pipelines were laid above ground across the route of a reindeer herd. The herd would not cross the pipeline or look for another route. Many died. Now pipelines are built with huge loops over the migration routes. This plan was developed at the Institute.

26

Soviet propaganda tries to promote harmony between native and immigrant people. In Yakutsk a militiaman stands in front of a huge billboard. It shows a dark-skinned Yakuti milkmaid hand-in-hand with a light-skinned Russian laborer.

The Yukagir

Tucked in the far northeastern corner of the Yakutsk Republic on the Arctic Sea is an area named the Kolyma District. It is governed from the town of Chersky. The city and surrounding area are the home of a small tribe of reindeer herdsmen called the Yukagir. For four thousand years they have tended their herds that roam the tundra just above the tree line.

The Yukagir number only 600 people, all of them members of about 100 families. They all work for the Nizhny Kolymsk State Farm which now covers the whole district.

For a month at a time the Yukagir live far out on the tundra. They care for moving reindeer herds that number up to 5,000 animals. On the tundra they live in reindeer-hide tents called *yarangas.* The tents are covered with furs and skins and heated by wood-burning stoves. Children are cared for in a boarding school set up in the town. Herdsmen keep a town home for the off-months when they are not working in the tundra.

The Yukagir are similar to the Eskimos. They are *shamanists*, or spirit worshipers. The "spirit of the deer" is called upon for a blessing when a guest comes or goes from the yaranga tent.

Grandmother Khodyan, at the left, is one of the few remaining *shamans,* **or spirit healers, in the Yukagir tribe. She is 110 years old. But she still chooses to live with her son and his family in the tundra. Every three days the family packs up its tents and follows the moving herds.**

29

The reindeer provides every need for the Yukagir. Reindeer meat is the main food. Hides provide shelter and clothing. Reindeer hair is used for mattress stuffing and the antlers provide medicine. A liquid from the glands of reindeer is also used as medicine. The Siberian north has more reindeer than people, and the herds are growing.

The Yukagir herds number 36,000 deer. Herdsmen receive a monthly salary of 200 rubles, about $250. Helicopters from Chersky are used to exchange herdsmen, to bring in needed supplies, and to take out the sick. Reindeer sleds provide ground transportation. A reindeer can cover one hundred miles in a day. It can run at twice the speed of a horse and cover a greater distance.

The Yukagir are a happy people who live a good life. They have the best of two worlds. For a month at a time they enjoy the peaceful isolation and the freedom of the wilderness. Every other month they can live in the modern comforts of the town at Chersky.

The tents of the Yukagir have two shapes. The round yurt is for sleeping, the teepee-like yaranga is for cooking and storage. When not in use, sleds are stacked against the double-thick reindeer skin wall.

This is Innokenty Khodyan and his children. They were photographed on the tundra about two hundred miles northwest of Chersky. The family of eight lives with a herd of 3,000 reindeer. The deer feed off moss found under the snow.

A Yukagir mother and child pose in front of their tent. Their clothing is made of reindeer skins, with fur trim.

Yukagir babies are put in fur bags that are carried on the sled or slung on the back. For warmth the fur is turned inside and placed next to the skin.

A young Yukagir is on a mission to get firewood for his family. He will travel about a hundred miles and be gone for nine hours. A reindeer can pull five times its own weight at speeds of fifteen miles an hour.

Reindeer bring huge profits to their owners, which are usually the Soviet State farms. In four years the owners can double the money they spend on the deer. One hundred thousand tons of reindeer meat are produced in the Soviet north each year.

Thanks to the reindeer herds, there is no food shortage in the Yukagir camps. Using a long knife, a herdsman kills the deer. But women are the butchers who skin and carve the animal. They work in temperatures of 22 degrees below zero. Only the body heat of the dead reindeer keeps their hands from freezing.

34

Freshly butchered reindeer is roasted over a wood fire in the cooking tent. It is tough and greasy. But it is tasty and gives more nutrition than beef.

The Evenki

Next to the Yakuti, the Evenki minority group covers the largest land areas of Siberia. But they number only about 25,000 people. Like the Yukagir they are mainly reindeer herdsmen and they, too, lead a nomadic life.

It is difficult to visit an Evenki camp. They can be reached only after several days' travel by reindeer sled or by helicopter travel. The herds are always moving and there is little communication with the herdsmen. The camps are often located only by a hit-and-miss air search.

One Evenki base camp was near Bolshoi Nimnyr, about fifty miles south of Aldan. I reached it only after a half-hour trip by helicopter from Aldan. The younger herdsmen were still eight miles away with the deer. But the senior herdsman, Ivan Pavlov, age 93, lived in the camp. The wives and the youngest children of the outbound herdsmen lived here too. A dozen sled reindeer and extra supplies were kept at the base camp while the herdsmen were out tending the reindeer.

The herd belonged to the Hatistir State Farm. The collective was located in the village of Hatistir, forty miles north of Aldan. Here permanent homes were kept for the herdsmen and their families. And here their children were sent to school.

Herdsmen work for three months. Then they spend twenty days at their village home. They always return to the same herd. They are paid 300 rubles, about $380, a month.

A base camp for Evenki reindeer herdsmen in the scrub forest near Aldan. For each herd, there will be several base camps like this one. Two weeks at a time will be spent at one camp, while the reindeer graze in the surrounding area. Then the herdsmen will move with the herd to another area for fresh grazing.

Ivan Pavlov, age 93, heads a family of Evenki herdsmen. Asked what his father did, he simply answered, "Herdsman, of course." He shuttles back and forth to the herd which is about seven miles away.

A *babushka,* or grandmother, pulls a tiny Evenki child through the snow at the base camp. The temperature was 22 degrees below zero on the day this picture was taken. But the women wore light clothing and no gloves!

Evenki children remain with their mothers at base camps until they are seven. Then they are sent to school at the State farm headquarters, a village 100 miles away.

Horsehair covers the bottom of the skis resting against the log cabin of an Evenki base camp. The herdsmen say the horsehair keeps the cold away from the feet. These may well be nick-named "hot skis."

After a ten-mile trip, reindeer pulling sleds are released from harness for a well-deserved rest. They carry great loads, up to 1,000 pounds. They can travel long distances at high speeds. The life span of a reindeer is ten years. Traditionally, herds always live and feed in the area of their birth. Their habits have remained unchanged for thousands of years.

Reindeer meat is easy to get all year in Siberia. Some is even shipped to Japan. The Soviets are steadily increasing the size of the reindeer herds. They now number two-and-a-half million. The target size is four million deer. Scientific research shows that the land can supply food for that many reindeer.

Helicopters are used in Siberia for emergency transportation. Many times they are the only means to quickly rescue sick herdsmen. Each herd has a short-wave radio that keeps in contact daily with collective farm headquarters.

Siberia's native groups are slowly learning the ways of the new Russian settlers. Future years may find them more integrated into the space-age pattern of living. But we can hope that their ancient heritage will not be destroyed in the process. Together, they form a unique culture which adds richness and variety to Siberian life.

Glossary

Aldan/ahl-DAHN/1) A city on the Aldan River in the Yakut Autonomous Republic in eastern Siberia; 2) a river in eastern Siberia which flows into the Lena River. 18

Angara River/ahn-guh-RAH/A river in southern Siberia which flows from Lake Baykal to the Yenisei River. 7

archaeologist/ar-kee-AHL-uh-jist/A person who studies about early cultures and peoples from the tools and buildings which they have left. 7

babushka/BAH-boosh-kuh/The Russian name for an old woman or a grandmother. 38

Bolshoi Nimnyr/buhl-SHOY neem-NEER/A small town in eastern Siberia. 36

Buddhist/BOO-dist/A person who believes in the Eastern religion started by the prophet Buddha. 10

Buryat/boor-YAHT/1) A tribe in southern Siberia; 2) the language of that tribe. 8
Buryat Republic: An Autonomous Soviet Socialist Republic near Lake Baykal. 10
Buryatia: The Buryat Republic. 14

Chersky/CHAIR-skee/A new seaport town in northeastern Siberia at the mouth of the Kolyma River on the Arctic Ocean. 29

collective farm/System of farming in which land, animals, and machinery are owned by the State. The farmers live together in a central village and go out to the fields to work. 12

Eskimo/ES-kim-oh/A race of people found in Greenland, Canada, Alaska, and northeastern Siberia. 9

Evenki/ih-VYEN-kee/1) A tribe of people in eastern Siberia; 2) the language of that tribe. 8

Genghis Khan/JENG-gis KAHN/A Mongol warrior who captured most of Asia and eastern Europe in the 19th century. 7

Hatistir/khah-tees-TEER/A small village in eastern Siberia in the Yakut Autonomous Republic. 36

Huns/An Asian people who invaded most of Siberia and eastern Europe in the fifth century. 7

Irkutsk/eer-KOOTSK/1) An Autonomous Soviet Socialist Republic in central Siberia; 2) the capital city of that Republic. 7

Kolyma District/koh-LEE-muh/An area in the northeastern corner of the Yakut Autonomous Republic. It is the home of the Yukagir. 29

kumiss/KOO-mees/An alcoholic drink made of fermented mare's milk. 11

lama/LAH-muh/A priest or monk of the Buddhist religion. 14

Lena River/LEN-uh or LEEN-uh/A major river in northern Siberia. 23

Magadan/mah-guh-DAHN/A seaport in far eastern Siberia on the Sea of Okhotsk. 9

Malta/MAHL-tuh/An area in southeastern Siberia which was invaded by the Huns in the fifth century. 7

Mongolia/mon-GOAL-ee-uh/A region of China. This area has now been divided into two regions: Outer Mongolia, now the People's Republic of Mongolis and a satellite of the Soviet Union; and Inner Mongolia, claimed by the People's Republic of China. 8

Mongols/A tribe of people from Mongolia. 8

nomadic/NOH-mad-ik/A person who travels across the country with his animal herds. 10

Olonkhosuts/aw-lawn-KHO-soots/Storytellers who used to wander from village to village, entertaining the Yakuti. 18

permafrost/An area where the ground is frozen all year round. 19

Pokrovsk/poh-KROVSK/A town on the Lena River in eastern Siberia. 19

prehistoric/Happening before the time of recorded or written history. 24

Sangara/sahn-guh-RAH/A town on the Lena River in northern Siberia. 23

Selenga Valley/SEL-eng-GAH/The valley of the Selenga River in central Siberia which flows into Lake Baykal. 11

shaman/SHAH-mun/A priest who uses magic to cure the sick, to discover secrets, and to control events. 29

shamanists: Those who believe in an unseen world of gods, demons, and the spirits of ancestors. 29

shashlik/SHASH-leek/A combination of meat and vegetables roasted on a metal skewer. 25

shish kebab/shish kuh-BAHB/A combination of meat and vegetables roasted on a metal skewer. 25

steppe/A large, grassy plain without trees. 10

taiga/TIE-guh/A region of large evergreen forests. 19

Tibet/tih-BET/A mountainous country southwest of China which is ruled by China. 17

tundra/TUN-druh/A treeless plain of the arctic areas. 8

Ulan-Ude/oo-LAHN oo DAY/A city near Lake Baykal in southern Siberia. 11

Union Republic/An administrative unit like a state. The Soviet Union has a federal government composed of fifteen Union Republics and a number of Autonomous Republics. 18

Ural Mountains/YOOR-ul/A mountain chain which runs north to south and divides the European part of the Soviet Union from Siberia. 8

46

Vilyuysk/VEEL-you-eesk/A town on the Vilyui River in east central Siberia. 18

Writer's Union/An association of Soviet writers. The Union plays a large role in deciding what kinds of books will be published and what authors will gain fame. 25

yak/yack/A shaggy-haired ox which lives in Tibet. 11

Yakut/yah-KOOT, pl. Yakuti/1) A tribe found in northeastern Siberia; 2) the language of that tribe. 7
Yakutsk Republic: An Autonomous Soviet Socialist Republic in northeastern Siberia. 26
Yakutia: the Yakut Republic. 18

Yakutsk/yah-KOOTSK/A city in the Yakut Republic on the Lena River. 7

yaranga/yuh-RAHN-guh/A Yukagir tent shaped like a teepee. It is made of reindeer hides and is used for cooking and storage. 29

Yukagir/YOU-kuh-geer/1) A tribe of people originally from Mongolia, now living in northeastern Siberia; 2) the language of that tribe. 8

yurt/yert/A dome-shaped tent made by Yukagir herdsmen. It is made of reindeer hides and is used for shelter when following the herds. 10

Howard Sochurek, a native of Wisconsin, is one of America's leading photographer-correspondents. During his distinguished career with *Time-Life* and as a free-lancer, he has circled the world more than a dozen times. Since 1958, when he served as *Time-Life's* first bureau chief in Moscow, he has made frequent trips throughout the Soviet Union, including the "New Frontier" regions of Siberia. In 1960 he served as a Nieman Fellow in Journalism at Harvard University, where he worked in the Russian Research Center. His most recent trip to Siberia was in February of 1973.

John deVisser, who along with Mr. Sochurek contributed many photographs for **The New Siberia** series, is a native of Holland. He emigrated to Canada in 1952 and began his photographic career a few years later. Over the past twenty years, his work has been published in most major Canadian and U.S. magazines. On photographic assignment, he has made two trips to the Soviet Union in recent years, including extensive coverage of Siberia.

Photographic Credits

John deVisser, 9 (bottom), 19, 21, 22, 25-28, 30-35, 45 (top right, bottom left and right).
Howard Sochurek, cover, 6, 9 (top), 11-17, 23, 24, 37-42, 43 (top left).